# HOW TO SELL ON AMAZON IN 2022

## *7 FBA Secrets That Turn Beginners Into Best Sellers*

### Matt Voss

## LEGAL

DISTRICT HOUSE

# CONTENTS

# READ THIS FIRST

As a thank-you for buying this book, I'd like to offer you the FREE Amazon FBA 7 Secrets Master Spreadsheet. Simply type the link below into your web browser:

*https://www.districthousepublishing.com/*

I **highly** recommend you use the Master Spreadsheet as a supplement to the book. I'll refer to it throughout the guide, and it's the best way to organize and maintain all of the product research and analysis you will be performing as an Amazon seller.

**If you're serious about using this book to learn how to make an income selling on Amazon, go to the link above and get the Master Spreadsheet today**.

In it, you will find:
- ❖ Step-by-step instructions on how to sell on Amazon FBA
- ❖ A tool for conducting product research and analyzing competition on Amazon
- ❖ A place to organize and maintain all of your supplier information, keywords, and product copy
- ❖ Bonus tips not included in the book

**Get the free Master Spreadsheet now!**

# INTRODUCTION

*"Find a job you like and you add five days to every week."* —H. *Jackson Brown, Jr.*

As you probably already know, countless people over the past several years have made fortunes selling through Amazon FBA, leaving the shackles of their day jobs behind and attaining freedom over their lives. Anyone hearing these success stories wonders if they could do the same. But the topic on everyone's mind is whether selling on Amazon has gotten too competitive. Let me address this concern very clearly:

**It is NOT too late to turn a profit and make an income selling on Amazon in 2022**

The reason for this is simple: *Amazon keeps growing.* In 2021, the company generated $470 billion in revenue, up 22% from the previous year. The year before the company grew another 38%, and the year before an additional 20%. What does this mean for new sellers?

**Even though competition is increasing on Amazon, the company is growing just as fast, if not faster, creating more and more opportunities for new sellers to enter the market**

*The Everything Store*, as it is commonly known, constantly expands into new markets and product categories, investing in its own infrastructure and distribution centers in order to enable its sellers not only to reach a wider customer base, but to do it more and more efficiently. Amazon *wants* its sellers to succeed—if they succeed, Amazon succeeds.

The point is, you should *not* be discouraged by the growing number of sellers and increasing competition on Amazon. The number of new opportunities more than offsets the rise in competition.

Before we move on, I'd like to briefly explain why I wrote this book. While Amazon boasts an impressive catalogue containing hundreds of millions of products, we all know from personal experience that not all of them are great products. Books are no exception. When I first started out as an Amazon seller years ago, I got my hands on every "How to sell on Amazon" guide there was, and I found that most of the books out there had one of two problems:

1. The "quick" or "easy" guides to Amazon FBA were for the most part disorganized and unedited. The ideas in them weren't organized in a way that would be helpful to a new seller. Nor was there much evidence of editing or revision, as the books were fraught with unclear meanings and grammatical errors.

2. The longer and more in-depth books went on for hundreds of pages with details that can easily overwhelm someone new to Amazon FBA. As someone who is a complete beginner, you don't need to be exposed to or slowed down by this mass of information. Most of it you will pick with experience. What's important in the beginning is that you learn the essentials for success.

And so I set out to write the best possible guide for new sellers, a book that can be read in a few sittings, and which covers everything you need to know in order to get started.

Now let's quickly go over how the book is structured.

Selling on Amazon essentially boils down to **three core tasks**:

1. Product Research

2. Product Sourcing
3. Product Listing

Everything you will do as a seller falls into one of these three categories, and so this book is organized to reflect this. The book contains three sections, one devoted to each core task.

## Product Research

Not only is this section first because product research comes before sourcing and building a listing, but because **product research is the most important core task**. It doesn't matter if you've mastered how to source your product and build an optimized listing—if you're not able to identify a profitable opportunity through product research, your business is doomed to fail.

In this section we will cover various ways to identify potential products, how to assess the competitiveness of a product niche, and how to create a unique competitive advantage. This section will demonstrate why product research is more an art than a science, and along the way you will learn the business theory necessary in identifying a product opportunity.

## Product Sourcing

The next core task is the one which tends to give new sellers the greatest anxiety. The thought of shipping goods from overseas, negotiating with foreign suppliers, conducting quality insurance, finding a freight forwarder, determining duties and taxes, etc.— the thought of everything involved in getting your products from a factory to an Amazon distribution center causes much worry and unease in prospective sellers.

But this is natural. In many ways, sourcing is the most straightforward part of the process. *If product research is the art, then product sourcing is the science.* Once you've successfully gotten your first shipment into Amazon, you'll have learned a lot about product sourcing—all of which will be covered in this section—

but you will also realize it's much more straightforward than how it may at first seem.

## Product Listing

Before your product lands at Amazon, you'll have created a product listing. This is your opportunity to showcase your product, along with its features and benefits. In this section we'll cover everything you need to do to optimize your product listing, including your images, title, description, keywords, and backend. We will also go over everything you need to do to grow and maintain your listing, including Pay-Per-Click (PPC) advertising, customer reviews, and inventory management.

So there you have it. If you're feeling overwhelmed right now, I totally get it. This can all seem like a lot to a new seller. Fortunately you have what I believe to be a great resource at your disposal now, and I encourage you to take notes and read this book twice or even three times if necessary. By the end of this guide, you will have learned everything you need to know to start selling your first successful product on Amazon!

Let's begin.

# SECTION 1: PRODUCT RESEARCH

*"People often say that motivation doesn't last. Well, neither does bathing - that's why we recommend it daily." —Zig Ziglar*

Before we dive into product research, I recommend you set up an **Amazon Seller Central** account (visit *"https://www.districthousepublishing.com/links"* for all links referenced in this book). This is a quick and easy way to start making progress towards becoming an Amazon seller. Speaking from personal experience, I've come to learn that it's important to stay motivated as an entrepreneur, and this is a great way to take that first step and motivate yourself to continue.

Seller Central is the web interface used by merchants to sell directly to Amazon customers. It's where you'll directly manage your business, from creating product listings to managing inventory. When signing up, new sellers often come across the following question:

**What is the difference between a Professional and Individual seller account?**

Eventually, assuming you plan on growing your business and making serious money, you will have the Professional plan. The Professional plan allows you to scale your business and avoid paying unnecessary fees for every product you sell. However, you do pay a monthly subscription fee of $39.99 per month, and so I recommend to **begin by opening an Individual seller account**, which is free, and then switching to a Professional plan once you are ready to sell your first product. That way you will avoid paying $39.99/month while you are determining what product to sell.

Signing up on **Seller Central** (visit "*https:// www.districthousepublishing.com/links*" for all links referenced in this book) is very simple. Remember to select the individual plan. We won't waste time going through the process step-by-step. There are plenty of videos and articles online that go through this, and our focus in this section is product research.

**Product Research is an art, not a science**

Product research does not lend itself easily to a step-by-step guide. There are no simple formulas or tools you can use to find great-selling products. Product research is an art, and success depends on many factors, including the seller's creativity and intuition. There are, however, certain tools and frameworks which will enable you to identify potential opportunities.

There are essentially two steps to product research:

1. **Generating a list of potential products**. In this first step you'll create a list of 10 products that you believe will sell well on Amazon.
2. **Product Validation**. Here you will validate with more rigorous analysis whether you should proceed with sourcing the products on your list.

We will be covering A LOT in this section. At some point or another you may feel lost, and that's OK. In due time, all of this will become second nature to you. If at any point you're not sure where you are in the process, refer to the outline below:

**Product Research Step-by-Step Outline**

1. Generate a list of 10 potential products
2. Perform Product Validation
    a) Product Analysis (Define your Competitive Advantage)

  i. Define the Market Focus
  ii. Define forms of Differentiation
  iii. Define the Relative Cost Position
  iv. Rank the 10 products in terms of the strength of your Competitive Advantage
 b) Competitive Analysis (5 Forces Analysis)
  i. Assess the Competitive Rivalry of your market
  ii. Assess the Potential of New Entry
  iii. Assess Supplier Power
  iv. Assess Customer Power
  v. Assess the Threat of Substitutes
  vi. Calculate a Competitiveness Score for each of your product's markets

All of this is outlined in greater detail in the **Amazon FBA 7 Secrets Master Spreadsheet**. Be sure to download it before you read further:

*https://www.districthousepublishing.com/*

We begin with how to generate a list of potential products.

## Product Research Step 1: Generating a list of potential products

There are limitless ways to find product ideas. The goal in this first step isn't necessarily to come up with a list of products you *know* will sell well, but to create a list of products you *believe* will sell well. Follow your intuition. Inevitably, not all of the products on your list are going to be winners. What might seem like a great opportunity now could later, upon analysis, prove to be a non-starter—or, alternatively, it could prove to be a great product that nobody has thought to sell.

First, I recommend you maintain your list of potential products in a spreadsheet. As we go on collecting more information about our products, a spreadsheet will allow for greater ease of comparison.

☆ **FBA Secret #1** ☆

*Only sell products on Amazon that have a proven market, with proven sales. Selling a completely new product will expose you to too much risk. When generating product ideas, ensure each product already has an existing market on Amazon.*

Here are **common methods Amazon sellers use to generate product ideas**:

❖ **Amazon.com.** The website itself is a great resource for product research. I encourage you to explore the immense product catalogue. Familiarize yourself with the product categories (e.g., Home & Kitchen, Office Products). Look for product ideas among Amazon's bestseller lists (visit *https://www.districthousepublishing.com/links*). A good way to do this is to drill down the product category to identify specific niches; for example, if you select "Home & Kitchen," you will see the best selling product for the *entire* department. But if you then select one of the Home & Kitchen *subcategories*, such as Home Décor, you will see the bestsellers for this subcategory. You can keep drilling down further and further to find products in more specific niches. **It is much easier to become a top product for a specific subcategory than it is for the entire parent category.** In determining a winning product, it is critical that you identify a specific market niche, but we will get into this in greater detail later in this section.

❖ **Alibaba.** When you begin product sourcing, you will likely use Alibaba.com. Alibaba is an interface that connects sellers to suppliers around the world. You will use this site to identify and communicate with foreign suppliers. Moreover, it can also be a great resource for product research. Simply go on the website and explore its various product categories. If you see a promising product, search for it on Amazon to gauge the existing market. As noted already, **select products that** are proven sellers and which have an existing market; do not sell new products that have no existing market. Selling a completely new product on Amazon will expose you to too much risk, as it would be very difficult to predict how a new product would sell.

❖ **Brick-and-mortar stores.** Every Amazon seller I've spoken to has gone to their local Walmart or Target in order to come up with potential products. It's a great way to expose yourself to new ideas you might not have discovered researching online. Bring paper and pencil. Walk around the store and write down the products that you think might sell well on Amazon. Make a note of the product itself, price, size, packaging, and any other distinguishing features. When you're back in front of a computer, research how these products are currently selling on Amazon.

❖ **Personal experience.** Think about what you've bought on Amazon and other retailers. What products do you use in your day-to-day? What around your house or apartment might make for a good product to sell on Amazon? Thinking about what you yourself use or are passionate about is a great way to identify products whose customers you understand, since you are among them! The more you understand your customers and their needs, the more value you can provide, leading to a superior product and greater sales.

❖ **Etsy and other niche e-commerce stores.** This little e-commerce website specializes in handmade items and craft supplies, and is a great resource for uncovering new product ideas. I myself have used the site to come up with product ideas that most Amazon sellers would never have thought of. Specifically, I recommend you find products on Etsy that would make for great *gifts*. Gift-giving is a colossal market. **If possible, you always want your product to be giftable.** Not only are you attracting customers buying for themselves, but for others, thereby increasing sales.

There are many other niche e-commerce sites, like Etsy, that you can use to generate product ideas. The main advantage of using sites like these is that you'll be able to find products that other sellers would never think to sell, and in an increasingly competitive space, it is critical that you identify unique products that will help distinguish you in the marketplace.

*A word of caution*: just because something sells well on a niche e-commerce site does not guarantee that it will sell well on Amazon. The very existence of these retailers is due to their specialization in certain types of products. For example, clothes and shoes are among the most purchased items online, though only about 20% of Amazon shoppers say they buy their wardrobe on Amazon (visit *https://www.districthousepublishing.com/links*).

**People simply do not shop on Amazon for certain types of products.**

As you consider which products to include in your list of ten (don't worry if it's not exactly ten), it may seem difficult to *know* whether or not a product is good enough to make the list. At the end of the day, it's your call, and some of it will rely on your intuition. There are, however, several considerations that will help in guiding your decisions:

❖ **Does the price point fall within the sweet spot of $15-40?**

  ➢ Items that fall under $40 are more likely to incur *impulse buys*. Customers generally don't spend too much time making a purchasing decision at this price range, making the likehood of a sale much greater.

  ➢ Items that you sell for less than $15 will likely have a profit margin that is too low. With Amazon FBA fees, shipping costs, and the cost of goods sold (what you pay the suppliers), you generally need to list your product for at least $15 in order to make a profit that is even worth your time. But I'll add a caveat to this: with increasing competition on Amazon, the price points that Amazon sellers generally avoid are becoming more and more attractive. So there are definitely exceptions to the $15-40 rule, and selling outside this range might allow you to sell in markets with relatively low competition.

➤ Items that sell for more than $40 are more likely to be heavy, and heavier items incur greater Amazon FBA fees, not to mention higher shipping costs. Amazon FBA fees depend on the weight of your product, and the fees can get quite steep for heavier items. In order to minimize fees, you should generally target items that are 2 pounds or less.

❖ **How can I enhance an existing product to ensure a competitive advantage?** Having a strong competitive advantage over your competitors is one of the most important factors—probably *the most important factor*—to your success on Amazon. And that is why during Product Validation (which is Step 2 of Product Research), you will analyze your competitive advantage in greater detail. While you are generating your list of potential products, it is important to start thinking about what your competitive advantage might be for a certain product. Here are some questions you should ask yourself:

➤ *How can I modify or enhance this product in a way that none of the existing sellers have?* Enhancements can take many different forms, including but not limited to enhancements to the product itself, packaging, listing (e.g., better pictures), bundling the product with other similar products, etc.

➤ *How easy would it be for new sellers to copy my product?*

Maybe you enter a market that is not too competitive and at first you enjoy a high profit margin, but if you haven't secured a strong competitive advantage, new sellers will inevitably swoop into your niche, create a similar listing, and drive sales away from your product. **The harder it is for competitors to copy your product, the better your product will sell long-term.**

➤ *What customer needs are existing sellers not satisfying?* A great way to discover potential product improvements is to read through existing reviews on Amazon. What are the customers complaining about? Why are some leaving less than 4-star reviews? What questions are they asking the seller? By solving a problem for customers that no existing seller has addressed, you are ensuring a competitive advantage.

❖ **How competitive is the product niche?** Concerns over too much competition is on every seller's mind. It used to be (back in the good old days) that you could pretty much enter any market and make a profit, even if your listing wasn't optimized or if your product wasn't especially unique. Now all of the "obvious" products that would sell well on Amazon are too competitive, and sellers are forced to seek out more obscure products and very particular niches. It has become more important than ever that a seller know how to assess the competitiveness of a product niche—that is why during Product Validation, along with identifying your competitive advantage, you will also perform a competitive analysis. But for now, here's **how you can gauge whether a product niche is too competitive**:

➤ If the average rating on the first page (when you search for a product on Amazon) is greater than 4, this indicates that customers are pretty satisfied with the existing product. It's not very likely that you can improve the product, and so you should avoid selling it.

➤ If on the first page there is more than one seller with thousands of reviews, or if the average number of reviews is more than a few hundred, avoid selling this product. This indicates that the market is highly competitive. Also, there should be 2-3 listings on the first page with less than 50 reviews.

➤ If there are more than a few thousand search results for your product, it is likely too competitive.

❖ **Other considerations**

➤ *Is it a gated product?* Certain types of products, such as lab equipment or food, require permission from Amazon before you begin selling. Ensure your product is not included in their list of gated categories and products (visit *https:// www.districthousepublishing.com/links*).

➤ *Is there low seasonality?* Your goal should be to find products that will sell year-round. Certain products, such as Halloween costumes, are highly seasonal and will not provide you with a steady stream of profits.

➤ *Is it a trademarked or brand-name product?* Avoid any products that are associated with trademarks or brand-names. Customers will flock to certain brands, and you don't want to be competing against a company like, say, Nike.

➤ *Is it a restricted product?* There are some products that can *never* be sold on Amazon. Ensure your product doesn't fall under Amazon's list of restricted products (visit *https://www.districthousepublishing.com/links*).

Finally, if you're still struggling to find product ideas, then I highly recommend you check out **101 Product Ideas for Amazon FBA**, now available on Amazon (visit *https://www.districthousepublishing.com/links*). In this book, I do something no Amazon seller has done before: I give you my own list of what I believe to be the best products to sell on Amazon in 2020.

Before we move on to Product Validation, let's quickly go over **Product Research tools**.

Wouldn't it be great to know your competitors' sales figures? To know exactly how many units they are selling per month? Obviously, this would be very powerful information, and there are tools out there that can provide it for you (not free of charge, of course).

You might be wondering how these tools obtain this data. In reality, all sales information is proprietary to Amazon, and they would never release sales data for specific listings. Tools such as **JungleScout** (by far the most popular one) use complex algorithms based on a multitude of variables to provide sales *estimates*. Still, these tools serve as very useful approximations of actual sales figures. I highly recommend starting out with the JungleScout Chrome extension. Using this tool, you can go on any product page on Amazon and see the monthly sales figures for each listing.

Say you were trying to decide between two products to sell—if all else were equal, wouldn't you pick the one that was selling, on average, thousands of units per month as opposed to hundreds? Clearly the first option is more lucrative. Product research tools provide this information for you and saves you the guesswork of attempting to estimate product sales yourself.

Once you've completed this first step of product research, you'll have a list of 10 potential products. Assuming you're using the Master Spreadsheet, record your products in the "Potential Products" sheet, specifically the Product Info table. In Step 2, we will fill out the Product Analysis and Competitive Analysis tables.

## Product Research Step 2: Product Validation

Now that you have your list of 10 potential products, you need to validate whether or not the items on your list are worth pursuing further. There are two types of analysis you have to perform in order to do this:

1. Product Analysis
2. Competitive Analysis

We have alluded to both already—now we will flesh out the exact steps needed to carry out the analyses. The first emphasizes delineating your unique position in the market. What specific niche are you targeting? What is your competitive advantage over other sellers? The second focuses on external factors. How competitive is the product niche? What are the competitive forces at play? We will cover each of these in turn.

**Part 1/2 of Product Validation: Product Analysis**

*"Obsess about customers, not competitors."*

*"If we can keep our competitors focused on us while we stay focused on the customer, ultimately we'll turn out all right."*

Both of the quotes above from Jeff Bezos, founder and CEO of Amazon, illustrate the primary reason for the company's incredible success: **an uncompromising focus on the customer**. Most sellers on Amazon make the mistake of doing the opposite, that is, being competitor-focused. It's simply human nature. It's natural to obsess over your competitors, focus on their products, and model your own after theirs with some marginal improvements. It's less natural and much more difficult to innovate—to find creative solutions to customer needs.

☆ **FBA Secret #2** ☆

*As an Amazon seller you should avoid complacency at all costs.*

A lot of sellers create a successful listing, start making some money, and think they can just leave their listing alone while it continues generating revenue for them indefinitely. This is called complacency, and it *kills* long-term profitability. Inevitably, other sellers will get wind of your product's success, create their own version, and cut away at your sales. To avoid this, a seller must constantly innovate their product according to changing customer needs and preferences.

Imagine the alternative: you're selling in a market in which all of the products are more or less the same. A seller lowers their price in order to capture a greater market share. Suddenly your sales plummet: customers *have no reason* to continue buying your product since it is more or less the same as the cheaper version. And so, to stay competitive, you lower your price—and before you know it you have entered what's known as a **Price War**. The saying goes that in war there are no winners. In the case of a price war, there is a winner: the customer. The customer enjoys paying low prices while sellers' margins have decreased to their lowest possible point. Clearly, this is not a position you want to be in.

Basically, the scenario above is meant to demonstrate that **you cannot expect to maintain success on Amazon by copying other people's listings**. In other words, you have to establish a competitive advantage.

**Competitive Advantage**

Your competitive advantage for any given product is defined by three different factors:

1. Market Focus
2. Differentiation

3. Relative Cost Position

As we go through each, make sure for each of your potential products you are defining each aspect of the competitive advantage in a spreadsheet or however you're recording your analysis.

*Market Focus*

In other words, who is your customer? Are they male or female? What's their general age range? What do they want from your product? It's critical that you know exactly who you are selling to and what their needs are.

Here is an example: say you are interested in selling *business card holders*. It's a very light product, so shipping and storage costs would be low. You search for the product on Amazon and you see that prices generally fall under the sweet spot of $15-40, but perhaps you can innovate the product somehow and thereby justify a higher price. This is when you have to stop and ask yourself: *who are my customers?* A lot of sellers skip this step and jump ahead to looking for suppliers on Alibaba. But if you asked yourself who your customers are, maybe you'd realize that most of the business card holders on Amazon are either meant for men or are unisex. What about *female* business professionals?

By thinking about our market focus, we have uncovered a potential customer group that is currently *underserved* on Amazon, and this means we have found an opportunity.

### ☆ FBA Secret #3 ☆
*By clearly defining market focus—the exact types of customers you are targeting—you're able to identify opportunities **before** your competition (e.g., customers who are currently underserved in the market)*

I'll repeat: *know your customer*. For most sellers, if you were to ask them who their customer is, the best they could come up with is something along the lines of "anyone who would own business cards." But this is too broad. By catering your product to specific types of customers, you will take market share from those sellers whose products are too general and are underserving certain customers.

For each product on your list, clearly define your Market Focus and record it in Column G of the "Potential Products" sheet of the Master Spreadsheet.

*Differentiation*

The second aspect of your competitive advantage is *Differentiation*. You can see how this goes hand-in-hand with Market Focus. Once you have defined your specific market focus, you will design your product to meet the needs of your customer.

Differentiation is by nature related to your competitors. You need to understand your competitors' product offerings in order to know how your product is different. Once you have defined your market focus, it's easy to research on Amazon's catalogue and find out how existing sellers are serving your niche.

There are many **ways you can differentiate your product** on Amazon:

❖ You can differentiate your product by your **product features**. There are countless ways to enhance your product itself in order to make it stand out. You can modify the product size, color, material, weight, shape, etc. Keep you Market Focus in mind. How are your modifications catering to your target customer?

❖ You can differentiate your product by **branding**. Branding is critical to long-term profitability. There are certain brands whose products you, as a customer, default to purchasing because you trust the brand will provide a certain level of quality. Sure, if you're just starting out, your brand is not going to become a household name like Nike or Coca-Cola anytime soon. But you can create the illusion that you are an established brand. Websites like **Fiverr.com** will connect you with freelancers who will design a product logo for you cheaply (15 or 20 bucks). You can then include this logo on your product, packaging, and/or listing, thereby increasing a potential customer's confidence that your product is of high quality.

❖ You can differentiate your product by your **packaging**. Packaging is an important aspect of the overall customer experience. Everyone has received something they ordered online with crude packaging, such as a cheap poly bag, that didn't quite align with the expectations that the product listing had set. Conversely, high-quality packaging such as a paperboard box with the company's logo on it can make a customer feel satisfied with their purchase before they even see the product. Additionally, visually-stunning packaging can increase the likelihood that purchasers leave positive reviews.

❖ You can differentiate your product by **bundling or adding a small gift**. This involves pairing your product with another product or small item that is somehow related. For example, say you are selling travel bags. What might someone who is travelling also need? Compression bags for clothes, neck pillows, toiletry bags, passport or document holders, etc. By selling items that are commonly purchased together, you are saving the customer the hassle of buying them separately, and for that you can charge a premium. *A word of caution*: it is relatively easy for competitors to copy a bundled product, and so bundling does not offer a sustainable competitive advantage. If you do plan to bundle, strongly consider differentiating your product in an additional way so as to ensure a long-term competitive advantage.

❖ You can differentiate your product by **product origin**. Many Americans are more likely to buy a product if it

were made in the U.S. In a recent survey (visit *https://
www.districthousepublishing.com/links*), 67% of adults in
the U.S. said they would *pay more* for a product if they
knew it was made domestically. Moreover, 52% said they
would rather pay $75 for a coat made in the U.S. than $50
for *the same* coat made overseas. These are very compelling
findings. If you are able to source your products from
the U.S., you can charge **a huge premium**, upwards of
50%. Also, with the recent tariff increases on Chinese
goods, sourcing domestically is becoming an increasingly
attractive option (we'll discuss this further in Section 2).

❖ You can differentiate your product by your **product
listing**.The one aspect of your listing that offers the
greatest potential for differentiation is your product
images. Customers highly weigh photos when making
purchasing decisions, and so having visually-stunning
photos can drastically increase sales. Hire a professional.
Ensure that your photographs showcase your product
features and how the product is meant to be used. Good
copy is less important, as customers often gloss over the
bullet points and product description, but it gives you an
opportunity to establish trust with the customer. Bad copy
—for example, a description clearly written by someone
who does not speak fluent English—is a surefire way to
turn customers away from your listing. We'll discuss in
greater detail how to build an optimized listing in Section
3.

Define 1-3 ways you plan to differentiate each of your 10 potential
products. Record this in Column H of the "Potential Products"
sheet of the Master Spreadsheet.

*Relative Cost Position*

Now that you have determined your Market Focus and how you
plan to differentiate your product, it's time to determine the third

and final aspect of your competitive advantage—price.

The price you set for your product should align with your Market Focus and Differentiation. For example, if you have created a product that's in some way superior to existing ones, then you can *charge more* than existing sellers. Here we see the value of targeting specific types of customers (ideally ones who are currently being underserved in the market) and creating a more valuable product through differentiation—we are able to charge a *premium*. Customers will often pay more for a superior product. It's that simple. You don't want to be one of the countless sellers forced to compete on price because they are all peddling the same products from China. To ensure long-term success on Amazon, you *must* sell unique products.

### ☆ FBA Secret #4 ☆
*The most important factor to long-term success on Amazon is maximizing long-term profits by maintaining a strong competitive advantage—i.e., providing a **unique** product offering*

Of course, a superior product does not necessarily mean a more expensive one. Perhaps you are selling a product that you're able to manufacture more cheaply than any other seller. In this case, you can pass cost savings over to the customer by lowering the price. This is, for example, how Walmart competes. Because they are able to source goods very cheaply, they can offer very low prices to customers.

Don't agonize over or waste too much time determining your initial price point. It is bound to change. Only when you begin selling the product can you perform tests to determine the ideal price (the price at which revenue is maximized). Say you are selling 100 units per month of a product at $10/unit. That's $1000/month in revenue. You wonder how much you'd sell if you increased the price to $15, and you find that you are now selling 75 units per month. Your new monthly revenue is now $1125, an increase of $125. Even though you are selling less units per month, you are making more money doing it. **Testing to find your product's ideal price point is critical to maximizing revenue.**

For now, pick a price point for each of your potential products and record this in Column I of the "Potential Products" sheet of the Master Spreadsheet.

At this point you've completed the product analysis. For each of your potential products, you have determined a competitive advantage, consisting of 1) Market Focus, 2) Differentiation, and 3) Relative Cost Position. Before you move on to the Competitive Analysis, **rank your products in terms of the strength of your competitive advantage**. Ask yourself:

1. How strong would my competitive advantage be if I entered the market today?
2. How likely would I be to sustain my competitive advantage in the future?

Record the rankings in Column F of the "Potential Products" sheet of the Master Spreadsheet.

We are nearly at the end of our product research. Soon we will decide which product to sell! But before we can make that decision, it is important that we perform a competitive analysis.

**Part 2/2 of Product Validation: Competitive Analysis**

In nearly every business school in America, you as a student are taught Porter's 5 Forces, which is a very useful tool for analyzing the competitive forces that affect a given industry. These forces are commonly used by businesses to assess the attractiveness of an industry or market, and can applied to markets on Amazon in determining their competitiveness. The 5 forces are:

1. Competition within the industry
2. Potential of new entry
3. Supplier power

4. Customer power
5. Threat of substitutes

*Competitive Force 1: Competition within the industry*

The first force refers to the level of competitive rivalry within an industry. The more competitors there are, and the more similar their products are, the lower the power of a given seller. Conversely, the lower the competitive rivalry, the more power you as a seller have to *increase prices*. Here are various factors to consider when assessing competitive rivalry:

❖ How many sellers on Amazon currently sell a product similar to yours?
❖ What is the average number of reviews for existing sellers?
❖ What is the average rating for existing products?

Assign a score of 3 (highly competitive), 2 (medium competition), or 1 (low competition) to each of your potential products. Here are some general guidelines you can follow in assigning this score (these are merely guidelines and should be taken with a grain of salt—they are based only on my experience as a seller and others might have different opinions):

❖ Number of sellers with similar product
  ➢ 1-5: Low
  ➢ 6-14: Medium
  ➢ 15+: High
❖ Average number of reviews for existing sellers
  ➢ 0-100: Low
  ➢ 100-300: Medium
  ➢ 300+: High
❖ Average rating for existing products
  ➢ 0-3: Low
  ➢ 3-4: Medium
  ➢ 4-5: High

Consider all three factors above, and assign a score (1, 2, or 3) to each product on your list. Add this to Column K of the Master Spreadsheet. You will then combine this score with scores you will be assigning based on the other four competitive forces to assess the overall competitiveness of your niche.

*Competitive Force 2: Potential of new entry*

This next force, also referred to as *Barriers to Entry*, is a very important consideration in assessing the competitiveness of a market. Essentially, we're asking how easy it would be for anyone to begin selling your product. It's obvious that the higher the potential of new entry (or the lower the barriers to entry), the more competitive the market. Factors that can *minimize* potential of new entry include:

❖ Products that are highly differentiated
❖ Brand names are important in purchasing decisions
❖ Initial investment is high
❖ Existing sellers have proprietary technology
❖ Accessing suppliers is difficult

Generally, as a new seller, unless you happen to have a lot of money to invest in your business at the outset, most of these factors will not be relevant to you. The key factor to focus on is the first, *Products that are highly differentiated*. Do existing sellers have differentiated products, or are they more or less the same? **The more differentiated products in the market are, the lower the potential for new entry.**

Considering the factors above, and weighing the first above all else, assign a score of 3 (high potential of new entry), 2 (medium potential of new entry), or 1 (potential of new entry) to each of your potential products. Trust your intuition. Don't spend too much time deliberating over whether the score should, for example, be a 2 or a 3. This is only 1 out of 5 competitive forces, and all five taken together (as we will do at the end) will give a reasonable approximation of the competitiveness of a market.

*Competitive Force 3: Supplier power*

The third force refers to how easily suppliers can raise the cost of goods. The key consideration in assessing this force is *the number of suppliers*. Think about it: the more suppliers there are, the more easily you can have them compete for your business, thereby lowering the price you pay for your products. Conversely, if there are only a few suppliers that can supply your product, you are forced to pay more if, say, they suddenly decide to jack up prices.

Here, assuming you plan to source your products from overseas, you can use Alibaba to get a sense of the number of suppliers that could potentially supply your product. Here are general guidelines you can use in assigning a score:

- ❖ 1-5 suppliers: 3 (High supplier power)
- ❖ 6-10 suppliers: 2 (Medium supplier power)
- ❖ 10+ suppliers: 1 (Low supplier power)

*Competitive Force 4: Customer power*

Customer power is somewhat similar to supplier power, in that the key consideration again is the *number* of customers. The smaller the client base, the more you depend on each customer to make a profit, thereby increasing customer power. The more customers there are, the less you depend on a few customers, and so you're more able to charge higher prices.

In assigning a score for customer power, it would be too difficult to estimate an actual number. Instead, here are example products that in my estimate would fall under each score:

- ❖ 3 (High customer power, few customers): badminton accessories, barber supplies, dental office supplies
- ❖ 2 (Medium customer power, medium number of customers): business card holders, flash lights, pressure cookers
- ❖ 1 (Low customer power, many customers): toilet paper,

phone chargers, scizzors

With these examples in mind, assign a score to each of your potential products.

*Competitive Force 5: Threat of substitutes*

The final competitive force refers to the potential for customers to use substitute products in place of yours. For example, if we are considering electric fans, a potential substitute for this product are portable air conditioning units. If there are no close substitutes, a seller's power in relation to the buyer is strengthened.

Again, here are some examples which you can use in assigning your scores:

- ❖ 3 (High threat of substitutes): beverages, transportation, cable subscriptions
- ❖ 2 (Medium threat of substitutes): electric fans, toys, irons
- ❖ 1 (Low threat of substitutes): binoculars, shower curtains, trading card sleeves

## We've finally come to the end of Product Research!

At this point you should have your list of potential products, ranked in order of the strength of your competitive advantage, and each should have five scores assigned to it from our competitive analysis. Now, add up the five scores (the Master Spreadsheet will do this for you automatically), and you should get a total between 5 and 15. Here is a simplified version of what your list might look like:

| Product | Competitive Advantage Rank | Competitiveness Score |
|---------|:---:|:---:|
| A | 1 | 10 |
| B | 2 | 9 |
| C | 3 | 14 |
| D | 4 | 10 |
| E | 5 | 13 |
| F | 6 | 7 |
| G | 7 | 6 |
| H | 8 | 7 |
| I | 9 | 8 |
| J | 10 | 9 |

As you can see in this example, the third highest ranked product in terms of competitive advantage has a Competitiveness Score of 14, which indicates that the product market is probably too competitive for entry. **I recommend you pick the top 3-5 products on your list that have a Competitiveness Score between 9 and 12.** Here's why:

❖ A Competitiveness Score of 13 or higher likely indicates that the market is too competitive, which means success is less probable
❖ A Competitiveness Score of 8 or lower likely indicates that the market is not competitive enough—fewer competitors might signal that the market is not attractive enough to encourage new entry
❖ A Competitiveness Score between 9 and 12 is the sweet spot: not too competitive but competitive enough that the market is attractive for new sellers

So now you have narrowed down your list of potential products to 3-5 products. Don't worry, I'm not suggesting you sell them all. The purpose of choosing 3-5 products is that sometimes during Product Sourcing, we might discover that a product would be too difficult or unfeasible to source, and so we have backups just in case.

Congratulations! You've completed the most important step in selling your first product on Amazon. **I realize Product Research is not easy**, and that we covered **a lot** in this section. But because we put in all this work up front, we have set ourselves up for success later on.

Moreover, while this book is meant to provide a concise overview of product research, you as a new seller still face *a substantial learning curve*. The fastest way to get through this learning curve, and to start selling ASAP is to **see first-hand how I find winning products to sell on Amazon**. And so I invite you to enroll in the *7 FBA Secrets Online Course* (see link below), where I will go through the entire process of selling on Amazon step-by-step, and find real products that we will then source and create product listings for.

If you're committed to starting an Amazon business, you need to go through the videos in the online course in conjunction with this book. All of the material covered in the book will be put into practice in the course, enabling you to absorb the material more quickly and start selling upon completion of the course. Don't hesitate! I highly recommend you enroll now before proceeding to the next section of this book. I'll see you there!

**Find the course link here**:

*https://www.districthousepublising.com/*

# SECTION 2: PRODUCT SOURCING

*"Language is the source of misunderstandings." —Antoine de Saint-Exupéry*

Given the trade war between the world's two largest economies and that underlying conflicts remain unresolved, sellers importing from China are still uneasy. Rises in tariffs increase the cost of sourcing from overseas, thereby affecting a seller's bottom line. Not all is bleak, however. Not all Chinese goods are affected by tariff increases, and even if they are, the lower cost of Chinese labor may still justify sourcing from there. Moreover, the current situation is creating opportunities to source elsewhere, including from other Asiatic countries and even domestically.

### ☆ FBA Secret #5 ☆
*The global-political climate is changing, and with change comes opportunity. Traditional sourcing methods are not as attractive as they once were. By sourcing through alternative means, sellers can get a leg up over their competition— specifically from Asiatic countries besides China and, to take advantage of the premium American shoppers are willing to pay for goods produced domestically, sourcing from the U.S.*

What's important is that we compare the costs of sourcing from various suppliers, and select one based on maximizing our profit margin while maintaining high product quality.

In this section we will cover:

1. Finding suppliers
2. What to include in your initial communication
3. Everything you should ask your supplier
4. What to include in an invoice
5. Shipping your product
6. How to select what products to source

During product sourcing, you'll collect a ton of information from your suppliers. The **Master Spreadsheet** provides a way of easily organizing all this. See the "Suppliers" sheet, and the "Instructions" sheet on how to fill it out.

## Part 1: Finding Suppliers

As a result of Product Validation, we have narrowed down our product list to 3-5 products. Now we must identify suppliers that align with our competitive advantage—that is, suppliers that can make our products according to our specifications.

Here are the **top five sourcing websites for Asiatic countries**, including a few important bullet points on each:

1. Alibaba.com
   a) The world's largest B2B sourcing portal
   b) Huge catalogue of products and suppliers
   c) Has a reputation for scams
2. DHgate.com
   a) Large catalogue of goods
   b) Usually has lower MOQs (Minimum Order Quantities)
   c) Payments finalized only when buyer confirms receipt of goods
3. GlobalSources.com
   a) Large catalogue that span over 240 countries
   b) Regular trade shows help facilitate trust with Chinese suppliers
4. Made-in-China.com
   a) Limited to Chinese suppliers

b) Clean, easy-to-navigate interface
5. China Suppliers (visit *https://
www.districthousepublishing.com/links*)
    a) Limited to Chinese suppliers
    b) Not a clean interface
    c) Claims to be government-backed

An alternative to sourcing from China while still reaping the benefits of cheap labor is to source from other Asiatic countries. The sourcing websites above specialize in Chinese suppliers, but some do include suppliers from elsewhere. Here are some alternative sites that specialize in other countries (visit *https://www.districthousepublishing.com/links*):

1. Vietnam
    a) Vietnam Manufacturers
2. Hong Kong
    a) HKTDC
3. Taiwan
    a) Taiwantrade
    b) B2B Manufacturers

Finally, there's the option of American sourcing. As mentioned in the previous section, sourcing from the U.S. is a great way to differentiate your product, as American customers are often willing to pay more for goods produced domestically. Plus, there are no tariffs, you deal with native English speakers, and shipping is typically faster. Here are a couple of popular **American sourcing websites** (visit *https://www.districthousepublishing.com/links*) :

1. Thomas Net
2. Maker's Row

Don't be overwhelmed by the multitudes of sourcing options. Keep in mind that it's better to have as many potential suppliers as possible so that you are better able to negotiate the cost of goods.

## *Part 2: What to include in your initial*

## communication

When communicating with suppliers, it's important to maintain a record of your conversation so that you can reference it later on. Many sourcing websites have Instant Messaging capabilities, which offer a convenient means of communication, the downside being that your conversations won't be saved. It's important to keep your suppliers honest, and sometimes they will say one thing one day and then contradict themselves the next. Minimize communication over IM as much as possible. And *always* begin communication through email.

Here's a template you can use in your initial email to suppliers:

**Subject**: RFQ for [Product Name]

**Body**:

Hi [Supplier Contact Name],

I'm [Your Name], founder and president of [Your Company Name], and I'm interested in receiving a quote for [Product Name].

In your response, could you please include:

1. Pictures of the product
2. MOQ, MOQ price, and prices for other order quantities
3. [Ask if they are able to customize the product according to how you plan to differentiate. Also ask how much these customizations would cost.]
4. How much does it cost to get a sample?
5. What are the shipping terms?

Thanks you very much. I look forward to hearing from you.

Best,
[Your Name]

President, [Your Company Name]

A few additional pointers:

❖ *Make your email stand out.* The contacts or salesmen you are reaching out to receive countless inquiries. Making your email stand out will increase the likelihood that they provide a thorough response.

❖ *Keep it simple.* The people you are contacting are likely non-native speakers of English, and so clear and concise language is all the more important in effective communication.

❖ *Keep it professional.* Remember that this is the first time you are communicating with a supplier, and so establishing a high level of professionalism early on is critical to maintaining it moving forward. Casually written instant messages or emails might result in suppliers taking you less seriously.

## Part 3: Everything you should ask your supplier

Following your initial email, there will likely be a long back-and-forth during which you'll determine whether the supplier is right for you.

Make sure that for each of your 3-5 validated products, you **reach out to as many suppliers as possible**. Ideally no fewer than 5. Around 8-10 is good, but more could never hurt. This may seem like a lot, but keep in mind that it would be a shame if the perfect supplier for the product you're envisioning were out there, and you never found them simply because you didn't put in the work.

Once you receive initial responses, you can begin weeding out those suppliers who:

❖ Take a long time to respond
❖ Don't answer all your questions
❖ Give vague or unintelligible responses

Hopefully, at least a few reply with detailed responses to all your questions and seem to be fluent enough in English.

Here are **the questions you should get answered as you proceed to communicate with suppliers**:

❖ *What payment options do you accept and what are the payment terms?* To pay for your sample(s), use PayPal. Most suppliers will accept payment in this method. It's a quick and secure way to pay for samples or even very small orders, but because PayPal charges a fee, it's not good for larger orders. When you finally order your first shipment, use an escrow service, which will hold your payment until you've confirmed that you received your order. Alibaba has its own escrow service called Trade Assurance, which is very helpful for first-time sellers wary of getting scammed.

❖ *What is the production lead time?* This refers to how long it would take from the moment you put in your order to when the order is ready to be shipped. Shorter lead times are obviously preferable for inventory management.

❖ *Could you provide quotes for FOB as well as DDP?* EXW, FOB, and DDP are three important Incoterms (International Commercial Terms) which specify who, the buyer or the seller, is responsible for what during the shipping process. EXW (Ex-Works) means the buyer is responsible for the shipment *as soon as it leaves the factory*. Obviously, this puts all of the responsibility on the buyer (you). When you are receiving quotes, they are typically for EXW. FOB (Free on Board) means the buyer is responsible once the shipment has reached the nearest port. And finally, DDP (Delivered Duty Paid) means the seller is responsible for everything, from the moment the shipment leaves the factory to when it arrives at its final destination (either an Amazon warehouse or your business if you plan to inspect and/or package units yourself). **DDP is an attractive option for first-time sellers**, as it is the simplest option, but it can also be more expensive since the factory selects the shipping company and method, and they might not choose the cheapest one. Get quotes from your supplier for all three and compare. If you find that EXW or FOB is significantly cheaper, you will need to hire a *freight forwarder* to make shipping arrangements for you, either from the factory or port.

❖ *Can you put my logo on the product or the packaging?* Creating a logo is a great way to begin establishing brand value. As noted in the previous section, websites like Fiverr connect you to freelancers who will design one for you. It's often very cheap to add your logo to packaging. Consider your logo along with other packaging options as a potential means of differentiating your product.

❖ *What are your packaging options?* When considering packaging options be sure to abide by Amazon's packaging and prep requirements. Related are the FBA product barcode requirements. (visit *https://www.districthousepublishing.com/links*). UPCs (your barcodes) are cheap and easy to obtain. Each of your products will require its own UPC, which can be purchased on *nationwidebarcode.com.* You can then send your barcodes to your supplier, who will apply your barcode on your packaging for you.

❖ *Do you know how to prepare packages for Amazon FBA? Have you shipped to an Amazon Fulfillment Center before?* Obviously, it's much easier to deal with a supplier who has had previous experience with Amazon FBA. An experienced supplier can even act as a FBA guide throughout the sourcing process. However, a question you might want to ask yourself is: if my supplier is so knowledgeable about Amazon FBA, what's stopping *them* from selling on Amazon? Many Chinese suppliers are getting smarter and realizing they can strengthen their margins by getting rid of the "middle man," in other words, *you*. Ensure that your product is sufficiently differentiated so that your supplier (and, more generally, any potential competitor) is less likely to sell the product themselves.

❖ *Do you refund fees paid for samples?* Many suppliers will do this if you proceed to order a shipment from them. Every dollar counts, and depending on how many iterations you go through in your product design, you may be paying for several samples, all of which you can ask to receive a refund for.

## *Part 4: What to include in an invoice*

Once you and your supplier come to an agreement on the shipping terms, the supplier will draft a **pro forma invoice**. A pro forma invoice is simply a preliminary bill of sale sent to buyers before shipment. Generally speaking, it should include the product specifications, cost of goods, and shipment information.

Over the course of your correspondence with the supplier, you will have discussed and agreed upon numerous points regarding your product, from exact specifications to shipping methods. **The pro forma invoice is your opportunity to list everything you agreed upon with your supplier.** Be specific. Make sure your supplier understands and agrees to every item in the invoice. If for some reason your supplier doesn't deliver according to your expectations, you'll be able to refer back to the invoice.

Below is a list of everything an invoice should include. Keep in mind that the supplier will draft the invoice, and that many (if not all) of these items will already be included.

❖ Supplier contact information
❖ Buyer information
❖ Shipping address
❖ Product specifications
  ➤ Material

- ➢ Size
- ➢ Weight
- ➢ Color
- ❖ Packaging specifications
- ❖ Price, order quantity, shipping terms (EXW, FOB, or DDP)
- ❖ Payment method
- ❖ Shipping cost
- ❖ Product lead time

**A note on product specifications**: be as specific as possible. Don't assume that your supplier will remember everything you agreed on over various emails and IMs. The more specific you are here, the less likely your supplier is to make a mistake in fulfilling your order.

## Part 5: Shipping your product

**When receiving a first shipment from a supplier, you should have the shipment sent to your residence or place of business**. This will give you an opportunity to inspect the product yourself and ensure it meets all specifications. Once you've done this, you'll ship your product to an Amazon fulfillment center. Amazon will connect you with their preferred carriers, which provide discounted shipping rates.

Once you've received a shipment or two from the supplier, you will have developed trust with them, and can have the supplier ship *directly* to a fulfillment center, saving you the extra step of shipping first to your place of business. All you need to do is send them the product labels.

## Part 6: How to select what products to source

After performing Product Research, we came up with a list of 3-5 products that passed our validation. Now, assuming you plan on starting out by selling one product, we finally need to choose which of our potential products to sell!

Since you've spoken to potential suppliers for each of the products on your list, you know how much it will cost to sell each product. Now we will select the best product to sell based on maximizing profit margin.

Profit margin is a simple calculation that takes into account price and cost.

## Profit margin per unit = Sales Price - Total Cost per unit

For example, if a product sells for $20, the cost to produce it is $8/unit, shipping is $2/unit, and FBA fees are $2/unit, then Total Cost per unit = 8 + 2 + 2 = $12/unit, and Profit margin = 20 - 12 = $8/unit. So for every unit you sell, you make $8. Now, if we want to calculate the profit as a percentage of sales, in other words, profit margin percentage, we perform the following calculation:

## Profit margin percentage = Profit per unit / Sales Price

Simply divide Profit per unit by Sales Price. In our example, since Profit margin is $8, and the Sales Price is $20, the Profit Margin percentage = 8/20 = 40%. Not bad! This means that for every unit you sell, you keep 40% of the sale.

Now, perform this calculation for the 3-5 product remaining on your list. No need to do this by hand. Amazon provides a Revenue Calculator (visit *https://www.districthousepublishing.com/links*), which will calculate profit for you and provide the FBA fees. Simply plug in the Item Price, Ship to Amazon cost, and Cost of Product for each of your potential products.

Now that we've calculated our profits, it's time to select a product to sell on Amazon! This is a bit more complicated than simply choosing whatever product has the highest profit margin. *Remember that the key to long-term success on Amazon is maximizing long-term profits by maintaining a strong competitive advantage.* Maybe one of your potential products has a profit of $10/unit today, but how likely are the profits to remain that way? Could they decline in the future? The key to answering this question is considering the strength of your competitive advantage. The stronger your competitive advantage, the more likely you are to maintain attractive returns in the long term.

Perhaps one of your products has a slightly lower profit of $8/unit. It's possible that this is the best product to sell. If you judge your competitive advantage with this product to be sufficiently stronger than your competitive advantage with the more profitable product, then, to ensure long-term success, sell the product with a lower profit margin.

A year from now, while you're maintaining a strong competitive advantage in your market and making $8/unit or more, competitors in the other market you were considering (with a $10 profit margin) may be facing lower margins as they struggle to differentiate themselves among the countless sellers with similar product listings.

# SECTION 3: PRODUCT LISTING

*"Sell the problem you solve, not the product."—Unknown*

In practice, there will be some overlap between sourcing and listing a product. Specifically, your product listing should be up and running *before* your first shipment arrives at Amazon's fulfillment centers. Once you decide on a product, you can begin creating the listing while you iron out the final shipping details with your supplier or while you wait for the order to be produced and shipped.

We will divide this final section into two parts:

❖ Part 1: Creating a product listing
❖ Part 2: Maintaining and optimizing a product listing

Part 1 will cover how to write effective copy, including the title, key product features, and description. It will also cover the backend and key considerations for your product images. Part 2 will cover how to optimize all of the aspects of your product listing once you begin making sales, including Pay-Per-Click (PPC) advertising.

## Part 1: Creating a product listing

Once you have all your product information ready, creating a new product listing on Seller Central is simple. Here are some key points to keep in mind when creating a listing:

1. Assuming you're doing private labeling, make sure you

are creating a *new* product listing. If you were a wholesaler, you'd be selling an existing product. But since you're selling a new product with a new ASIN or UPC code, so you should choose the option to create a new product listing.

2. Keep your Brand Name general and not specific to your product as you will be selling different types of products in the future.

3. Select the most accurate category and subcategories for your product. Obviously, it's important that customers be able to find your product, and it may be difficult or impossible to do so if your product is in an inappropriate category.

4. You can always go back and edit any aspect of your product listing, so it's fine to only fill out the required fields at first and then go back to complete the listing information.

Creating the listing itself is easy, but writing effective copy for the listing is a little more challenging. Here are **the four elements of product copy on Amazon, in order of decreasing importance:**

1. Title
2. Bullet points
3. Product description
4. Backend

The title is the most important aspect of your product copy. Customers use it to identify your product, and so Amazon weighs this heavily when considering how relevant your listing is to what a customer is searching for. Since the title is most important, it's critical to add your most relevant **keywords** to the title. Keywords are search terms customers use to find the products they want to buy.

For example, here are a few keywords that are relevant to sports pinnies:

❖ Scrimmage vests
❖ Mesh jerseys

❖    Practice pinnies

A customer might use any of these search terms to find your product. **When performing keyword research, it's important to imagine all the various ways a customer might search for your product**. You should keep a list of the most relevant keywords for your product, ranked in order of decreasing relevancy.

Don't worry, you won't have to come up with every keyword on your own. There are countless tools out there that help determine the most relevant keywords for your product. Here are some that I recommend:

❖    **Google Keyword Planner**. This in my mind is the best way to get started with keyword research. Firstly, it's free. Moreover, Keyword Planner will give you a list of keywords relevant to your product, along with their search volume, so you can see how often people are searching for a given keyword.

❖    **Sonar.** Also free, this Google extension uses complex algorithms to provide keywords used specifically by Amazon shoppers.

❖    **Merchant Words**. This tool, though not free, helps develop keyword phrases to use on Amazon.

Be sure to refer to the Master Spreadsheet, where you can easily maintain a list of relevant keywords and write the product copy.

Once you have a list of relevant keywords for your product, you can begin writing the product copy. Here are the key points to keep in mind:

❖    **Title**
   ➢    *Don't stuff keywords*. Many sellers will create long and complicated titles in order to work in as many keywords as possible. In reality, keyword stuffing hurts your product listing, as it becomes less

optimized for SEO (Search Engine Optimization)—in other words, customers not looking for your product will see it (because you included their search term in your listing) and not click on it. Amazon will detect this and lower your product ranking. In general, include only relevant keywords in the product copy. For the title, focus on creating an attractive title using 1-3 of the top keywords.

➢ *Follow Amazon's style guide.* For each category, Amazon provides a guide specifying how you should name your product. Be sure that you're not breaking any of the guidelines.

❖ **Bullet points**
  ➢ *Create concise bullets.* Keep in mind that shoppers glance through product copies, spending mere seconds in making their purchasing decisions. You get five bullet points to outline your key product features —keep them short and to the point, highlighting the key benefits of the product. Try to work in relevant keywords, but your priority should be to outline concisely the product features.

  ➢ *Consider customer objections.* If there's any reason why a customer might hesitate to buy your product, address them directly in the bullet points. Put yourself in their shoes: what are the most important considerations in making a purchasing decision? What problems do similar products have and how is yours better?

❖ **Product description**
  ➢ *Tell a story.* This is your last chance to entice the customer. Get into their head, relate to their lives, and address any final objections. How will their lives be improved from using your product as opposed to an inferior one?

> *Use HTML formatting.* As far as product copy goes, this is the least important aspect that shoppers will see (the backend is hidden). You'll be lucky to have more than a few seconds to grab your reader's attention. No one wants to read a long paragraph, and so it's critical to make the description as reader-friendly as possible. HTML allows you to modify the formatting of the product description by adding **bold lettering**, *italics*, and <u>underlines</u>, as well as spacing. It's easy to implement, and there are countless resources out there that show you exactly how to do it.

❖ **Backend**
> *Include only relevant keywords.* Back in the day, there was essentially no limit to the backend (hidden keywords that customers don't see), and sellers would stuff as many keywords into the backend as possible, even if they weren't relevant. Recent changes by Amazon have made it so you are considerably more limited in the number of keywords you can include. This means you should include only relevant keywords that you haven't already mentioned in the title, bullet points, or description. **Don't repeat keywords**. If you've already included it in the product copy, there's no point in including it in the backend.

Keep in mind that the product copy will change in the future as you optimize your product listing. We will cover this in greater detail in Part 2.

The other, and probably more important, aspect of the listing are the **product images**.

Studies have shown that online shoppers form their first impression of a product within milliseconds. Clearly, they're forming their judgements based on your product images. **Captivating photos are critical to making sales, and can in**

**themselves serve as a form of differentiation.** Sometimes you can copy an existing seller's listing almost exactly, improve the images, and drive away their sales simply by having superior photos.

Here are the key points to consider when obtaining product images:

1. **Your main image should include only your product with a white background**—do not include text, logos, or any other content; this rule is included in Amazon's Product Image Requirements (visit *https://www.districthousepublishing.com/links*)

2. **Minimize white space** and make your product image take up as much of the frame as possible; extra white space is unattractive

3. **Hire a professional**. Find a local photographer, ideally someone who has done product images before. Ask if they're able to take photos of your product with a solid white background as well as in a natural setting. Also, are they able to hire models?

4. **Ensure product images are high quality**—lower quality images are not only less attractive but do not include zoom-in features

5. **Your images should tell a story**: how is your product meant to be used? How does it fill a need or solve a problem for the customer? Secondary or additional images do not have the same restrictions as the primary image; feel free to include text and infographics to enhance the images

6. You are allowed seven to nine images on your product page: *use all of them*

7. Consider infographics as a way of highlighting your product features; free-lancers on Fiverr can create these for you very cheaply

When hiring a professional, keep in mind that you are making a long term investment in your product. It will probably cost you at least a couple hundred dollars to obtain professional, high-quality images for your product, and possibly even more if you hire models or have photos done in a natural setting. Assuming you are seeking to sell a product for the long haul (which I hope you are), a few hundred dollars spent upfront is a trifle compared to your long-term profits.

At this point, your listing is up-and-running, with an effective copy and high-quality images. Once your first shipment arrives at Amazon and you begin making sales, you need to consider how to optimize the listing, which we'll now cover in Part 2.

## Part 2: Maintaining and optimizing a product listing

The key to optimizing a product listing is to test variations of each aspect of the listing, which is known as **split testing** (also referred to as A/B testing). We'll go over how to split test each component of the product listing in turn.

### ☆ FBA Secret #6 ☆
*Split testing is one of the easiest and most effective ways of increasing your conversion rates, thereby converting page visitors into buyers.*

*Split testing product images*

Though you are allotted seven to nine images (Amazon allows you to upload nine, but generally only seven of them appear on the listing), you will likely receive many more from your photographer. Moreover, depending on whether you have infographics or edited images, you may have many more options to fill just seven image slots. So how do you decide which images to include?

It's not necessary—in fact it's very unlikely—that you perfectly select the images that will lead to the greatest number of sales. When selecting your images in the beginning, use your best judgement. Then, as you begin making sales, you can experiment with variations in your product images to see which lead to more sales—this is essentially how split testing works.

Generally, a split test should last at least a week. A week to two weeks is advisable. Let's consider an example:

Say you are currently averaging $100 per day in sales for a certain product, and you're wondering whether a different main image would result in greater sales. We'll call your current main image *Image A*. To perform split testing, change the main image to one you think will lead to greater sales, Image B, and watch sales over the next 1-2 weeks. What were the average daily sales for Image B? If it's greater than 100, great! You've uncovered an optimization in your listing. If not, that's OK. This may be indicative of an already optimized main image. Just be sure to change your main image back to Image A once split testing is complete.

The above example shows **how split testing essentially works**:

1. You have an idea for a listing optimization
2. You modify the listing accordingly and sit back for 1-2 weeks
3. At the end of the testing period, you measure average daily sales in order to see whether the hypothesized optimization actually resulted in greater sales

A few important notes on split testing:

❖ *Test only one change to the product listing at a time.* Making multiple changes at once will lead to inconclusive results. Say you tested two changes at once, and your average daily sales decreased, so you decided not keep either of the changes. It's possible that both changes led to lower sales. But it's also possible one change actually contributed to *greater* sales while the other lowered sales by a higher degree. By split testing multiple changes at once, you miss out on potential listing optimizations.

❖ *Account for confounding variables.* A confounding variable is anything that distorts the results of your split testing. For example, say you tested a new product image during the holidays. You might see a spike in sales, and falsely conclude that it was due to the new image, when in fact seasonality was the true cause of the sales fluctuation. Be sure to perform split testing in conditions that minimize confounding variables.

❖ *A sample size that is too large is always preferable to one that is too small.* 1-2 weeks is advisable for split testing; however, you may run into scenarios in which you just don't have enough sales data to make any definitive conclusions. If this is the case, extend the sample size a week at a time until you've obtained statically significant data.

*Split testing product copy (Keyword optimization)*

Split testing the product copy follows the same essential logic as described above.

Keep in mind the priority of each element of the product copy:

1. Title
2. Bullet points
3. Product description
4. Backend

Be sure to focus your efforts on optimizing the title before anything else. Once you feel you've done so, you can continue moving down the list. Here are two common optimizations to a product title:

❖ *Keyword ordering.* You should already have your top 1-3 keywords in the product title. Amazon sets greater priority to what comes earlier in the title, so ideally your top keyword should be the first one that appears in your title. But what if you're not sure what your top keyword actually is? Play around with the order of the keywords in the title and see if there's a significant change in sales.

❖ *Different keywords.* Experiment with your list of relevant keywords. Just because a specific keyword phrase is highly searched does not mean it's suitable for your product. Similarly to how we drilled down during product research to identify our specific market focus or niche, the product title should use specific keywords in describing your product. This will enable customers searching for your specific product to find it more easily.

Besides listing optimization, there are some final key considerations to keep in mind related to maintaining a product listing. These include PPC, inventory management, and customer reviews. We'll now cover each of these in turn.

*Pay-Per-Click (PPC) advertising*

PPC advertising is essentially a way of pushing your product to the customer. You've probably noticed that when you buy something on Amazon, the first few results will typically say "Sponsored." The sellers of these product are running a *PPC campaign.* If you click on their sponsored product, the seller pays Amazon a small fee—hence the name *Pay-Per-Click*—whether you end up buying the product or not.

That last part is very important: **you pay Amazon a fee every time someone clicks on your sponsored ad, whether they end up buying your product or not.** Don't worry about one of your competitors sitting around all day and clicking on your ads— Amazon will detect this and not charge you. Moreover, you can set daily limits on your PPC campaigns so that you never get charged more than a certain amount.

There are entire books out there devoted to this topic. Here we will cover the essentials.

An Amazon PPC campaign works like this:

1. From Seller Central start either a *manual* or *automatic* campaign. In an automatic campaign, Amazon does all the work for you. Based on your product listing, Amazon will decide if your product is relevant to what a customer is looking for and then list your product as a sponsored ad (so that it's one of the first results that come up in a customer search). Later, in the *Search Term Report* that Amazon provides, you can see what searches your product came up for and how often shoppers clicked on your ad. In this way, **automatic campaigns show you what Amazon thinks you are trying to sell**. This is very useful information, and it's possible that the Search Term Report will give you keyword ideas you haven't already thought of.

Alternatively, you can set up a manual campaign, which is more involved. Here, you choose the keywords you want your ad to be displayed for. This is where your keyword list comes in handy. For all the keywords you want to advertise for, you set a bid (Amazon provides you recommended bids). Additionally, you can set exactly how a customer search needs to match a keyword you're bidding on—this option is known as *match type*, and can be set to Broad, Phrase, or Exact.

There are plenty of online resources that get into the specifics of the pros and cons of each match type. Basically, Broad will cause your ad to show up for customers whose search is more loosely related to your product keyword, while for Exact, your ad comes up only if a customer searches your *exact* keyword. Ideally, you should maximize the number of Exact match types in your campaign so that your ads are *targeted* and you are not wasting money on customers clicking on your product who are in fact looking for something else. The benefit of the other match types is that the Search Term Report could potentially provide new keyword ideas.

2. Once you run the campaign, you will begin bidding with other sellers on whatever keywords you selected for your campaign (or in the case of automatic campaigns, Amazon chooses the keywords for you). The highest bidder wins. Say your bid for the keyword "back scratcher" is $2.50, and the next highest bid is $1.50. Because you are the highest bid, your ad shows up when someone searches "back scratcher," and if they click on your ad, you basically pay the next highest bid (plus one cent, so in this example you'd pay $1.51).

3. On any given day, your PPC campaign will continue to run until it has reached its daily limit. (Be sure to **set daily limits** unless you want to be surprised by a massive PPC charge.) Once the limit has been reached, your ads will cease to come up for all customer searches. Additionally, your PPC campaign can end on a certain day if you set an end date when creating the campaign.

As the number of new sellers and products continues to grow, it becomes increasingly difficult to run a profitable paid-advertising campaign. The bids necessary to win ad space are getting higher, and so to justify paying more for PPC, sellers need to be very strategic in their advertising efforts. Here are **the keys to running a successful PPC campaign:**

❖ *Ensure your listing is highly optimized **before** you run a PPC campaign.* If your listing doesn't contain high-quality images and an effective product copy, it doesn't matter if you are winning bids—online shoppers are not very likely to click on your ad and even less likely to make a purchase. Additionally, make sure the keywords you're advertising for are included in the product copy.

❖ *Use **negative keywords** to control advertising costs.* By setting negative keywords, you prevent your ad from showing up for certain customer search terms. This is very useful when you discover you're bidding for search terms that are unrelated to your product or will definitely not lead to a sale. For example, say you are selling a product for which customers are sensitive to the color, and your product is yellow. You can list as negative keywords "purple [product name]" or "brown [product name]" so that you avoid paying unnecessary ad dollars targeted towards customers who wouldn't buy your product anyway.

❖ *Know your break-even ACoS*. ACoS (Advertising Cost of Sale) simply represents how much you pay for PPC. It's a ratio, calculated as a percentage of sales. For example, if a product sells for $10, and it costs $1 in PPC advertising to get it sold, ACoS is calculated as 1/10 = 10%. Moreover, the **break-even ACoS is the profit margin before advertising**. This is an important concept, so let's dive deeper.

In a previous section we learned how to calculated profit margin: profit as a percentage of sales. So say after the cost of goods sold, shipping, and FBA fees, you're making a 30% profit margin. As a result, *the highest ACoS you can have without losing money is 30%*. At 30% you break even (meaning you don't make or lose money). Once you know the break-even ACoS for a given product, you can gauge whether a particular keyword is worth advertising for.

For example, if the ACoS for a particular keyword is 50% and your break-even ACoS is 30%, you are losing money bidding on this keyword. To lower the ACoS, simply lower your bid for this keyword. But this isn't always the best move. If the **conversion rate** (percentage of product page visitors who make a purchase) for this keyword is very high, consider maintaining a high bid for this keyword since you are making sales, which will drive up your **organic ranking** (where your non-sponsored product listing shows up for a customer search).

It's worth paying more than the break-even ACoS if it results in your product coming up on the first page. Obviously, you can't operate on a loss forever. Once you reach your goal (of getting on the first or even second page) lower or even pause your bids, as you can rely now on making sales without having the advertise.

☆ **FBA Secret #7** ☆

*In assessing the effectiveness of a PPC campaign, the conversion rate for a particular keyword you are bidding on is just as important as the associated ACoS. High conversion rates often justify a high ACoS, even if the ACoS is greater than the Profit Margin before advertising.*

*Inventory management*

As you begin selling larger volumes on Amazon, the importance of a strong inventory management strategy becomes critical.

**Effective inventory management essentially ensures that you are meeting customer demand while at the same time NOT tying up cash in inventory when you could be using it to invest in other products.**

Not enough inventory will result in you losing customers and slipping in ranking. Too much inventory ties up money in unsold goods and results in extra storage costs. And so a solid inventory management strategy aims to maintain *Just In Time* inventory, meaning inventory levels are optimized to exactly match customer demand.

Here are **four tips to achieve Just In Time inventory**:

1. *Know your turnover rate.* Inventory turnover rate refers to the length of time it takes to sell your entire inventory. You should always have a good idea about how many units you are selling a day. You should use this to forecast when your inventory will run out. Seller Central has a built-in tool that tracks sales and recommends when you should replenish inventory.

2. *Know your production lead times.* Lower production lead times are obviously ideal for maintaining Just In Time

inventory. Whatever your lead time, you should have a good sense of the duration from the moment you put in an order to when the shipment arrives at Amazon.

3. *Plan for seasonality.* Different products experience different seasonalities. Many experience sales spikes during the holidays. Your understanding of your product's seasonality will strengthen over time, but if you're just starting out, forecast seasonality to your best ability. Consider similar products and research how their sales fluctuate throughout the year.

4. *Lower demand if necessary.* If you find yourself nearing a scenario in which you've run out of inventory, it's better to raise the price or less aggressively advertise your product so as to decrease demand. It's better to have lower sales in the short term than to run out of inventory—the latter would seriously affect your product ranking.

*Customer Reviews*

It goes without saying that positive customer reviews are a prerequisite for increased sales. And so naturally, there are many sellers out there who will do anything to get them, which include illicit tactics that are forbidden by Amazon, such as using fake accounts or email append services to obtain customer emails. Doing anything that's not allowed by Amazon's rules and guidelines is indicative of a gap in a seller's long-term thinking. Is it worth obtaining one or even a few 5-star reviews if you're risking getting your account permanently suspended? Be wary of straying from Amazon's guidelines. If you suspect you're in a gray area or think there's even a chance you're doing something that could get your account suspended—don't do it. It's not worth your business essentially coming to an end.

There are, however, several permissible ways to obtain more reviews on Amazon:

❖ *Modify your product or packaging so as to encourage customers to leave reviews.* Wouldn't you be more likely to leave a positive review for a product that comes in a sleek box that includes a product logo than something that comes in a simple poly bag? A product that delivers on its promises and that comes in high-quality packaging is much more likely to receive positive reviews.

❖ *Include packaging inserts.* Package inserts are a cheap and effective way to encourage customers to leave reviews. Here you can get very creative as to your message to the customer. It's best to make them visually appealing and include your logo. Consider hiring a freelancer to design the insert for you.

❖ *Request reviews from customers you provided customer service for.* If you've supported a customer during their purchase and they had a positive experience, be sure to ask them to leave a review. Happy customers are usually willing to provide positive reviews.

❖ *Do product giveaways and discounts.* Amazon Giveaways is a program that allows you to give away products for free or at discount. It's a great way to encourage customers to leave reviews. Steep discounts in general lead to more sales and increase the likelihood of getting reviews.

Congratulations! We've reached the end of the book!

We started from knowing very little about Amazon FBA to finding product ideas, validating potential products by defining a long-term competitive advantage and assessing competition; we covered product sourcing, including everything from finding suppliers to shipping, and finally we learned how to create and optimize a product listing.

If you haven't already, I highly recommend you enroll in the *7 FBA Secrets Online Course*. While this book serves as a quick and handy reference guide for selling on Amazon, nothing will accelerate your learning and set you up for success quite like the course. Through hours of instructional content, you will see the concepts covered in this book put into practice, and **watch as I perform product research and uncover real opportunities for selling on Amazon**. So enroll now, and we'll continue our journey there!

Visit *districthousepublishing.com* to receive a free coupon for the course, or go to the course directly using the link below.

**Course Link:** https://www.udemy.com/course/fba-secrets/?referralCode=B44F6B1A27CBCAFC7325

My hope is that this book has instilled in you the fundamentals of growing a successful business not only on Amazon, but beyond. The concepts you've learned here can be applied to any business— Amazon is only the beginning. Good luck!

# APPENDIX

## The Consolidated List of FBA Secrets

### ☆ FBA Secret #1 ☆

*Only sell products on Amazon that have a proven market, with proven sales. Selling a completely new product will expose you to too much risk. When generating product ideas, ensure each product already has an existing market on Amazon.*

### ☆ FBA Secret #2 ☆

*As an Amazon seller you should avoid complacency at all costs.*

### ☆ FBA Secret #3 ☆

*By clearly defining market focus—the exact types of customers you are targeting—you are able to identify opportunities **before** your competition (e.g., customers who are currently underserved in the market)*

### ☆ FBA Secret #4 ☆

*The most important factor to long-term success on Amazon is maximizing long-term profits by maintaining a strong competitive advantage—i.e., providing a **unique** product offering*

### ☆ FBA Secret #5 ☆

*The global-political climate is changing, and with change comes opportunity. Traditional sourcing methods are not as attractive as they once were. By sourcing through alternative means, sellers can get a leg up over their competition— specifically from Asiatic countries besides China and, to take advantage of the premium American shoppers are willing to pay for goods produced domestically, sourcing from the U.S.*

## ☆ FBA Secret #6 ☆

*Split testing is one of the easiest and most effective ways of increasing your conversion rates, thereby converting page visitors into buyers.*

## ☆ FBA Secret #7 ☆

*In assessing the effectiveness of a PPC campaign, the conversion rate for a particular keyword you are bidding on is just as important as the associated ACoS. High conversion rates often justify a high ACoS, even if the ACoS is greater than the Profit Margin before advertising.*

Made in United States
North Haven, CT
26 September 2024

57961290R10039